Our Cherished Things

a family record

These we love are our most cherished things!
Patricia Sprinkle

created by Patricia Sprinkle

Printed in the United States of America, 2013.

Library of Congress Cataloging-in-Publication Data

Sprinkle, Patricia
   Cherished Things: A Family Record/Patricia Sprinkle;
   illustrations by Lindy Burnett; graphic design by Natalie Nelson.

I S B N 978-0-9884829-0-6

   1. Journal/family record 2. Heirlooms 3. Genealogy/family history

Cherished Things:
Our Family's Heirlooms

Stories of our family's most cherished possessions
and memories that cling to them,
so that future generations can cherish them as well.

prepared with love by: _____

Item: _____

Description: _____

_____

_____

Why it is precious to us: _____

_____

_____

_____

_____

_____

If the item has been valuated:

VALUE $ _____ VALUATION DATE: _____

VALUATOR: _____

LOCATION OF VALUATION DOCUMENTATION: _____

Item: _____

Description: _____

_____

Why it is precious to us: _____

_____

_____

_____

_____

If the item has been valuated:

VALUE $ _____ VALUATION DATE: _____

VALUATOR: _____

LOCATION OF VALUATION DOCUMENTATION: _____

Item: _____

Description: _____

_____

_____

Why it is precious to us: _____

_____

_____

_____

_____

_____

If the item has been valuated:

VALUE $ _____ VALUATION DATE: _____

VALUATOR: _____

LOCATION OF VALUATION DOCUMENTATION: _____

Item: _____

Description: _____
_____

_____

Why it is precious to us: _____

_____

_____

_____

If the item has been valuated:

VALUE $ _____ VALUATION DATE: _____

VALUATOR: _____

LOCATION OF VALUATION DOCUMENTATION: _____

Item: _____

Description: _____

_____

_____

Why it is precious to us: _____

_____

_____

_____

_____

_____

If the item has been valuated:

VALUE $ _____ VALUATION DATE: _____

VALUATOR: _____

LOCATION OF VALUATION DOCUMENTATION: _____

Item: _____

Description: _____

_____

_____

Why it is precious to us: _____

_____

_____

_____

_____

_____

If the item has been valuated:

VALUE $ _____ VALUATION DATE: _____

VALUATOR: _____

LOCATION OF VALUATION DOCUMENTATION: _____

Item: _____

Description: _____

_____

_____

Why it is precious to us: _____

_____

_____

_____

_____

_____

If the item has been valuated:

VALUE $ _____ VALUATION DATE: _____

VALUATOR: _____

LOCATION OF VALUATION DOCUMENTATION: _____

Item: _____

Description: _____
_____
_____

Why it is precious to us: _____
_____
_____
_____
_____

If the item has been valuated:

VALUE $ _____   VALUATION DATE: _____

VALUATOR: _____

LOCATION OF VALUATION DOCUMENTATION: _____

Item: _____

Description: _____

_____

_____

Why it is precious to us: _____

_____

_____

_____

_____

_____

_____

If the item has been valuated:

VALUE $ _____ VALUATION DATE: _____

VALUATOR: _____

LOCATION OF VALUATION DOCUMENTATION: _____

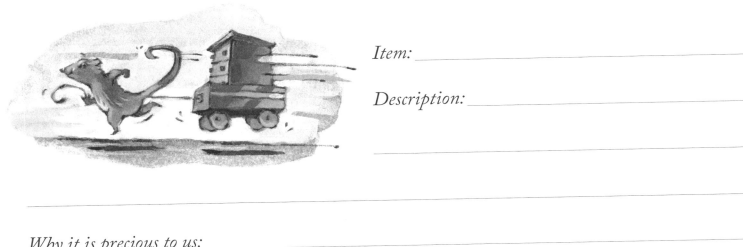

Item: _____

Description: _____

_____

_____

Why it is precious to us: _____

_____

_____

_____

_____

_____

If the item has been valuated:

VALUE $ _____ VALUATION DATE: _____

VALUATOR: _____

LOCATION OF VALUATION DOCUMENTATION: _____

Item: _____

Description: _____

_____

_____

Why it is precious to us: _____

_____

_____

_____

_____

If the item has been valuated:

VALUE $ _____ VALUATION DATE: _____

VALUATOR: _____

LOCATION OF VALUATION DOCUMENTATION: _____

Item: _____

Description: _____

_____

_____

Why it is precious to us: _____

_____

_____

_____

_____

If the item has been valuated:

VALUE $ _____ VALUATION DATE: _____

VALUATOR: _____

LOCATION OF VALUATION DOCUMENTATION: _____

Item: _____

Description: _____

_____

_____

Why it is precious to us: _____

_____

_____

_____

_____

_____

If the item has been valuated:

VALUE $ _____ VALUATION DATE: _____

VALUATOR: _____

LOCATION OF VALUATION DOCUMENTATION: _____

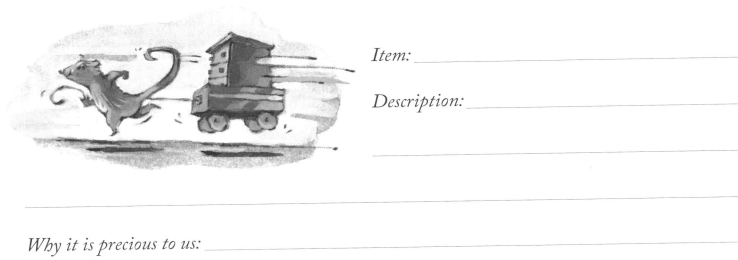

Item: _____

Description: _____

_____

_____

Why it is precious to us: _____

_____

_____

_____

_____

If the item has been valuated:

VALUE $ _____ VALUATION DATE: _____

VALUATOR: _____

LOCATION OF VALUATION DOCUMENTATION: _____

Item: _____

Description: _____

_____

_____

Why it is precious to us: _____

_____

_____

_____

_____

_____

_____

If the item has been valuated:

VALUE $ _____ VALUATION DATE: _____

VALUATOR: _____

LOCATION OF VALUATION DOCUMENTATION: _____

Item: _____

Description: _____

_____

_____

Why it is precious to us: _____

_____

_____

_____

_____

_____

If the item has been valuated:

VALUE $ _____ VALUATION DATE: _____

VALUATOR: _____

LOCATION OF VALUATION DOCUMENTATION: _____

Item: _____

Description: _____

_____

_____

Why it is precious to us: _____

_____

_____

_____

_____

_____

If the item has been valuated:

VALUE $ _____ VALUATION DATE: _____

VALUATOR: _____

LOCATION OF VALUATION DOCUMENTATION: _____

Item: _____

Description: _____

_____

Why it is precious to us: _____

_____

_____

_____

_____

If the item has been valuated:

VALUE $ _____ VALUATION DATE: _____

VALUATOR: _____

LOCATION OF VALUATION DOCUMENTATION: _____

Item: _____

Description: _____

_____

_____

Why it is precious to us: _____

_____

_____

_____

_____

_____

_____

If the item has been valuated:

VALUE $ _____ VALUATION DATE: _____

VALUATOR: _____

LOCATION OF VALUATION DOCUMENTATION: _____

Item: _____

Description: _____

_____

_____

Why it is precious to us: _____

_____

_____

_____

_____

_____

If the item has been valuated:

VALUE $ _____ VALUATION DATE: _____

VALUATOR: _____

LOCATION OF VALUATION DOCUMENTATION: _____

Item: _____

Description: _____

_____

_____

Why it is precious to us: _____

_____

_____

_____

_____

_____

If the item has been valuated:

VALUE $ _____ VALUATION DATE: _____

VALUATOR: _____

LOCATION OF VALUATION DOCUMENTATION: _____

Item: _____

Description: _____

_____

Why it is precious to us: _____

_____

_____

_____

_____

If the item has been valuated:

VALUE $ _____ VALUATION DATE: _____

VALUATOR: _____

LOCATION OF VALUATION DOCUMENTATION: _____

Item: _____

Description: _____

_____

_____

Why it is precious to us: _____

_____

_____

_____

_____

_____

If the item has been valuated:

VALUE $ _____ VALUATION DATE: _____

VALUATOR: _____

LOCATION OF VALUATION DOCUMENTATION: _____

Item: _____

Description: _____

_____

Why it is precious to us: _____

_____

_____

_____

_____

_____

If the item has been valuated:

VALUE $ _____ VALUATION DATE: _____

VALUATOR: _____

LOCATION OF VALUATION DOCUMENTATION: _____

Item: _____

Description: _____

_____

_____

Why it is precious to us: _____

_____

_____

_____

_____

_____

_____

If the item has been valuated:

VALUE $ _____ VALUATION DATE: _____

VALUATOR: _____

LOCATION OF VALUATION DOCUMENTATION: _____

Item: _____

Description: _____

_____

Why it is precious to us: _____

_____

_____

_____

_____

If the item has been valuated:

VALUE $ _____ VALUATION DATE: _____

VALUATOR: _____

LOCATION OF VALUATION DOCUMENTATION: _____

Item: _____

Description: _____

_____

_____

Why it is precious to us: _____

_____

_____

_____

_____

_____

_____

If the item has been valuated:

VALUE $ _____ VALUATION DATE: _____

VALUATOR: _____

LOCATION OF VALUATION DOCUMENTATION: _____

Item: _____

Description: _____

_____

Why it is precious to us: _____

_____

_____

_____

_____

_____

If the item has been valuated:

VALUE $ _____ VALUATION DATE: _____

VALUATOR: _____

LOCATION OF VALUATION DOCUMENTATION: _____

Item: _____

Description: _____

_____

_____

Why it is precious to us: _____

_____

_____

_____

_____

_____

If the item has been valuated:

VALUE $ _____ VALUATION DATE: _____

VALUATOR: _____

LOCATION OF VALUATION DOCUMENTATION: _____

Item: _____

Description: _____
_____

Why it is precious to us: _____
_____
_____
_____
_____
_____
_____

If the item has been valuated:

VALUE $ _____ VALUATION DATE: _____

VALUATOR: _____

LOCATION OF VALUATION DOCUMENTATION: _____

Item: _____

Description: _____

_____

_____

Why it is precious to us: _____

_____

_____

_____

_____

If the item has been valuated:

VALUE $ _____ VALUATION DATE: _____

VALUATOR: _____

LOCATION OF VALUATION DOCUMENTATION: _____

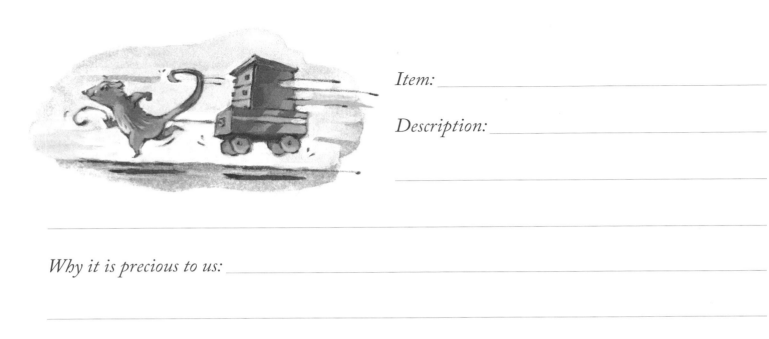

Item: _____

Description: _____

_____

_____

Why it is precious to us: _____

_____

_____

_____

_____

If the item has been valuated:

VALUE $ _____ VALUATION DATE: _____

VALUATOR: _____

LOCATION OF VALUATION DOCUMENTATION: _____

Item: _____

Description: _____

_____

_____

Why it is precious to us: _____

_____

_____

_____

_____

_____

_____

If the item has been valuated:

VALUE $ _____ VALUATION DATE: _____

VALUATOR: _____

LOCATION OF VALUATION DOCUMENTATION: _____

Item: _____

Description: _____

_____

_____

Why it is precious to us: _____

_____

_____

_____

_____

If the item has been valuated:

VALUE $ _____ VALUATION DATE: _____

VALUATOR: _____

LOCATION OF VALUATION DOCUMENTATION: _____

Item: _____

Description: _____

_____

_____

Why it is precious to us: _____

_____

_____

_____

_____

_____

If the item has been valuated:

VALUE $ _____ VALUATION DATE: _____

VALUATOR: _____

LOCATION OF VALUATION DOCUMENTATION: _____

Item: _____

Description: _____

_____

_____

Why it is precious to us: _____

_____

_____

_____

_____

_____

If the item has been valuated:

VALUE $ _____ VALUATION DATE: _____

VALUATOR: _____

LOCATION OF VALUATION DOCUMENTATION: _____

Item: _____

Description: _____

_____

_____

Why it is precious to us: _____

_____

_____

_____

_____

_____

_____

If the item has been valuated:

VALUE $ _____ VALUATION DATE: _____

VALUATOR: _____

LOCATION OF VALUATION DOCUMENTATION: _____

Item: _____

Description: _____

_____

_____

Why it is precious to us: _____

_____

_____

_____

_____

If the item has been valuated:

VALUE $ _____ VALUATION DATE: _____

VALUATOR: _____

LOCATION OF VALUATION DOCUMENTATION: _____

Item: _____

Description: _____

_____

_____

Why it is precious to us: _____

_____

_____

_____

_____

_____

If the item has been valuated:

VALUE $ _____ VALUATION DATE: _____

VALUATOR: _____

LOCATION OF VALUATION DOCUMENTATION: _____

Item: _____

Description: _____

_____

_____

Why it is precious to us: _____

_____

_____

_____

_____

_____

If the item has been valuated:

VALUE $ _____ VALUATION DATE: _____

VALUATOR: _____

LOCATION OF VALUATION DOCUMENTATION: _____

Item: _____

Description: _____
_____
_____

Why it is precious to us: _____
_____
_____
_____
_____
_____
_____

If the item has been valuated:

VALUE $ _____ VALUATION DATE: _____

VALUATOR: _____

LOCATION OF VALUATION DOCUMENTATION: _____

Item: _____

Description: _____

_____

_____

Why it is precious to us: _____

_____

_____

_____

_____

_____

If the item has been valuated:

VALUE $ _____ VALUATION DATE: _____

VALUATOR: _____

LOCATION OF VALUATION DOCUMENTATION: _____

Item: _____

Description: _____

_____

_____

Why it is precious to us: _____

_____

_____

_____

_____

_____

If the item has been valuated:

VALUE $ _____ VALUATION DATE: _____

VALUATOR: _____

LOCATION OF VALUATION DOCUMENTATION: _____

Item: _____

Description: _____

_____

_____

Why it is precious to us: _____

_____

_____

_____

_____

If the item has been valuated:

VALUE $ _____ VALUATION DATE: _____

VALUATOR: _____

LOCATION OF VALUATION DOCUMENTATION: _____

Item: _____

Description: _____

_____

_____

Why it is precious to us: _____

_____

_____

_____

_____

If the item has been valuated:

VALUE $ _____ VALUATION DATE: _____

VALUATOR: _____

LOCATION OF VALUATION DOCUMENTATION: _____

Item: _____

Description: _____

_____

_____

Why it is precious to us: _____

_____

_____

_____

_____

If the item has been valuated:

VALUE $ _____ VALUATION DATE: _____

VALUATOR: _____

LOCATION OF VALUATION DOCUMENTATION: _____